Franz Karg   **Solid-Wood Cabinet Construction**

Solid-Wood Cabinet Construction

Franz Karg

70 contemporary designs with details

The Taunton Press

Library of Congress Cataloging-in-Publication Data

Karg, Franz.
    [Massivholzmöbel. English]
    Solid-wood cabinet construction: 70 contemporary
designs with details / Franz Karg.
            p.   cm.
    Translation of: Massivholzmöbel.
    ISBN 3-421-02972-5 (Germany)
    1. Cabinet-work.   II. Title.
TT197.K3613   1991
684. 1'6—dc20   90-26591
                                                      CIP

ISBN 0-942391-97-7

First published in Germany as
Massivholzmöbel: Konstruktions- und Ausführungsbeispiele
(© 1989 Deutsche Verlags-Anstalt GmbH, Stuttgart)

The Taunton Press
Box 5506
63 South Main Street
Newtown, CT 06470-5506

TAUNTON
BOOKS &VIDEOS

...by fellow enthusiasts

oreword

Look in the dictionary under the word "solid" and you will find such synonyms as firm, sturdy, strong, durable, whole (not hollow) and pure.

This gives us a sense of what is meant by "solid wood" and also helps us to understand why solid-wood case furniture has increased in popularity in recent years.

The market for solid-wood products is in part made up of people who have maintained, or rediscovered, an appreciation for nature, and for natural materials as opposed to man-made materials. And wood is, of course, a natural material; it is "pure" and "whole." Because of its durability, it has great intrinsic value when fashioned into furniture. Solid-wood furniture becomes more and more beautiful with age. If it is damaged, it can be repaired or restored, which invalidates the charge that solid wood is wasteful of material.

The fact that solid-wood furniture does not needlessly add to our garbage dumps stands in stark contrast to the wastefulness of short-lived, mass-produced furniture. In addition, with the use of solid wood, there is little or no danger of exposure to the possible harmful materials in synthetic furnishings.

It takes a long time for a change in attitude to occur. Solid wood has a warmth, a liveliness and an individual quality, springing from its prominent texture and natural graining, that can help to bring about such a change.

Perceptive furniture makers and furniture vendors are quick to notice changing customer demands. Designers and technicians must face the challenge that the production of solid-wood furniture presents.

An enlightened designer appreciates the wealth of possibilities that working in solid wood can offer. For example, an exposed structural detail, such as a finger joint or dovetail batten, can often be used as a decorative element. This is only of value, however, if it retains its original function, in this case, to connect individual parts or to ensure the alignment of doors and panels. Consider also the numerous design possibilities that cabinet locking mechanisms in solid wood offer.

An appropriate choice of material from a design and structural viewpoint can, for example, heighten the effect of a cabinet front. The natural versatility of solid wood, in terms of texture, color and figure, can be put to use in almost endless ways. Fine-grained wood can be placed in contrast to beautifully figured wood; exposed joints, if they are worked out appealingly, can attract attention; interesting light-and-shade effects can be produced by using pale wood.

Technicians ask themselves many questions: Are traditional production methods compatible with modern machinery? Do we really have the long-established technical knowledge of former generations of cabinetmakers? How practical is it to make solid-wood furniture? Is the raw material that is cut today for quite different applications suitable for the production of such furniture? Technicians also have to come up with ideas about how to dry wood for end-grain elements. We can find solutions to these problems, and the old handcrafted techniques can be learned. Although we should not simply copy old designs or follow the ideas of our forefathers when they appear meaningful, it would be unwise to disregard well-tried construction methods entirely.

This book presents numerous examples of the way traditional methods of construction can be combined with contemporary design. Young would-be cabinetmakers, happy to be experimenting, have followed my suggestions and, through hard work, have realized their ideas. I am especially grateful to them.

I hope that they will have the opportunity to use what they have learned in their professional lives. I wish them much success.

Franz Karg

Publisher's note: All measurements used in the drawings are metric.

Contents

Board Construction

This style of furniture making, especially the face design, is certainly the most Spartan, if not the easiest to build. The problem of keeping solid-wood boards in alignment is usually overcome by using battens fastened perpendicular to the boards.

These battens are normally mounted on the inside face, but they can be incorporated into the front design as decorative elements.

An alternative is to insert splines through the boards, which lets you further divide the face into individual boards, opening up new design possibilities.

Cross rails or end-grain rails can also be used instead of battens to keep the board faces level. This again opens the way for a number of design variations.

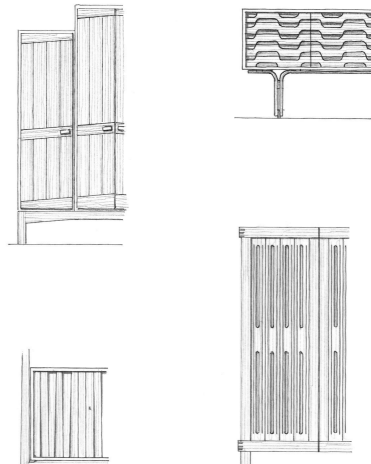

Living-room cabinet in Douglas fir. The feathers that are partly visible on the door and drawer faces are stained blue. Cross rails at the top and bottom of the doors and battens dovetailed into the inside face keep the boards in alignment. The door-latch mechanism is comprised of a sliding wood handle.

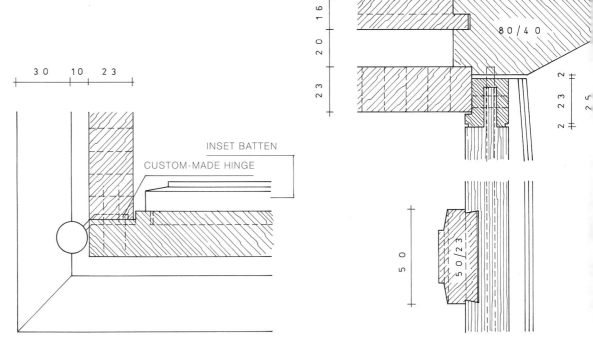

INSET BATTEN

CUSTOM-MADE HINGE

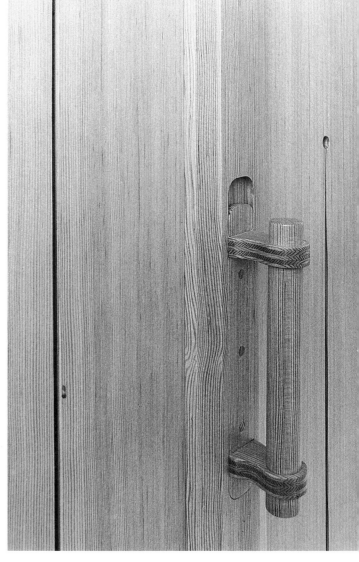

The bevels on the doors and drawer faces of this sideboard and wall cabinet produce a particularly fine light-and-shade effect. Using light wood, such as spruce, further accentuates the effect. Chip-carved battens on the inside of the doors are revealed when the sideboard opened.

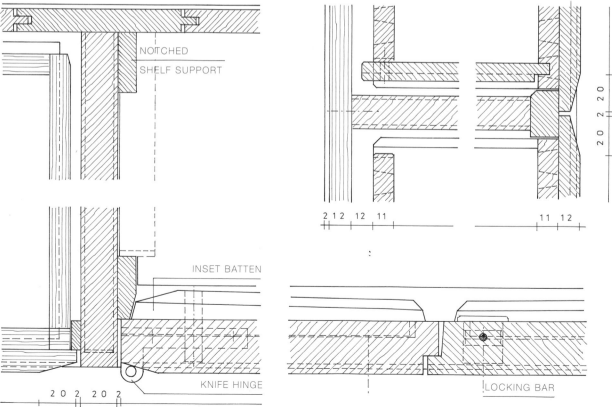

NOTCHED
SHELF SUPPORT

20 2 20

2 12 12 11

11 12

INSET BATTEN

KNIFE HINGE

LOCKING BAR

20 2 20 2

"Austerity of form" is the hallmark of this double-sided desk with two document cabinets. All corner joints are finger-jointed, and the cabinet casters are made of laminated wood. The plain beechwood used for this piece was chosen carefully and is particularly well suited to the design.

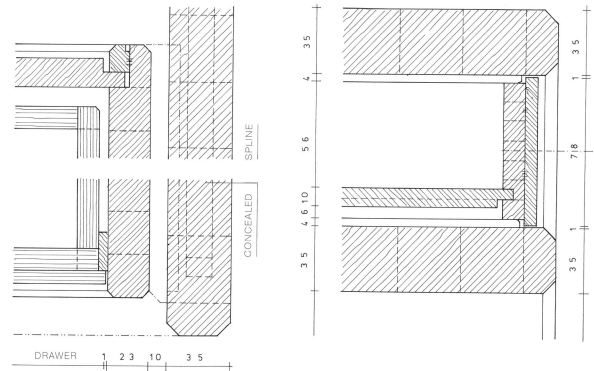

SPLINE

CONCEALED

DRAWER   1   2 3   10   3 5

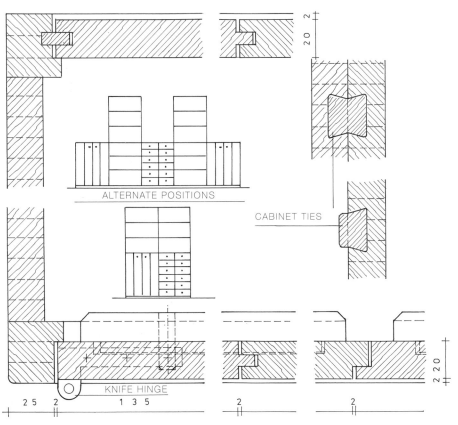

ALTERNATE POSITIONS

CABINET TIES

KNIFE HINGE

2 5   2   1 3 5   2   2

INSET

BATTEN
3 3 / 2 1

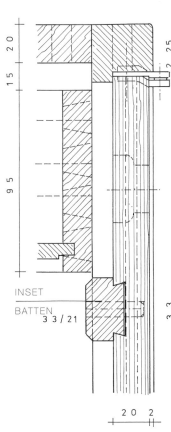

The interchangeable parts of this modular beech unit are joined to each other with interesting dovetail joints. Inserted splines hold the two boards of each door together.

Simple board construction was used for this spruce and larch bookcase in a children's bedroom.

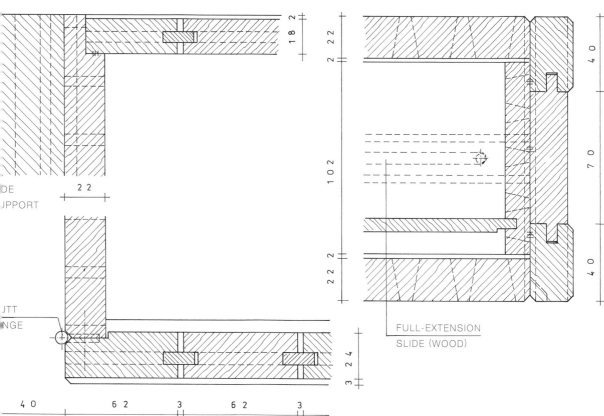

DE
UPPORT

2 2

UTT
NGE

FULL-EXTENSION
SLIDE (WOOD)

Desk of fine-grained spruce and natural leather. Both the larger work table and the side table for typewriter or computer turn on a metal pivot above the lower cabinet. This means that the work station can be used in a variety of positions. Inserted splines keep the boards of the doors in alignment.

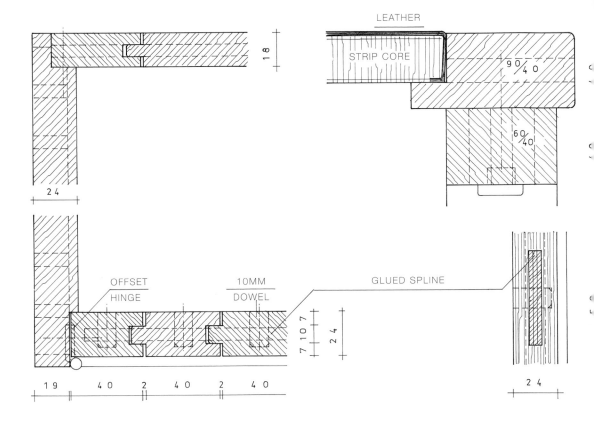

19

This glass cabinet in spruce and cherry features board construction throughout. The sides are rabbeted, and the board doors are built with inserted splines. All exposed edges are rounded.

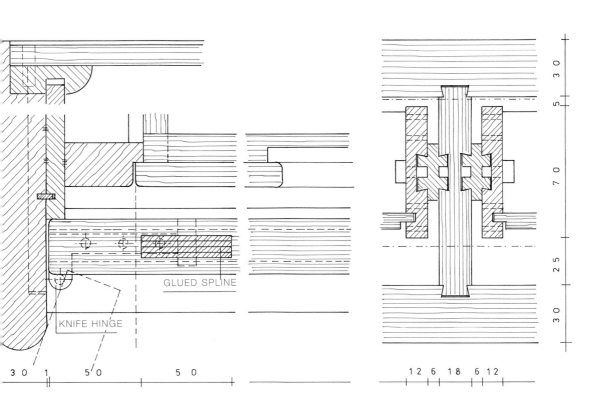

GLUED SPLINE

KNIFE HINGE

3 0 1   5 0   5 0

1 2 6   18   6 12

The cutouts in the boards of the doors are sandblasted, accentuating the effect of depth on this spruce sideboard.

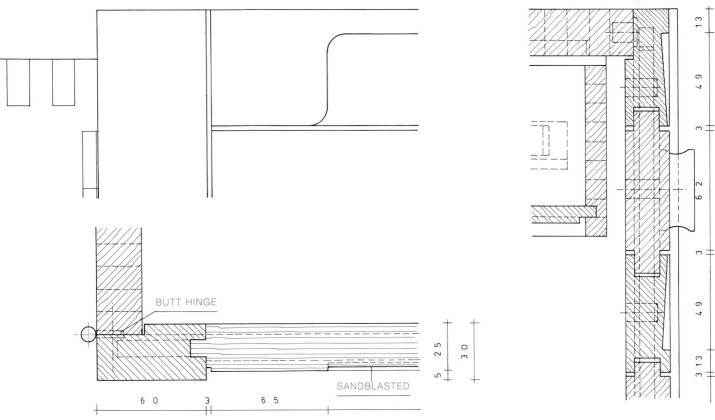

BUTT HINGE

SANDBLASTED

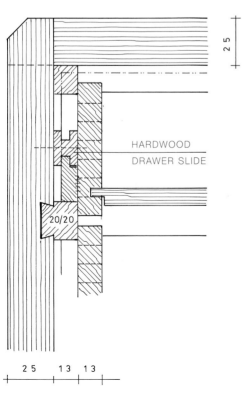

25

HARDWOOD
DRAWER SLIDE

20/20

2 5   1 3   1 3

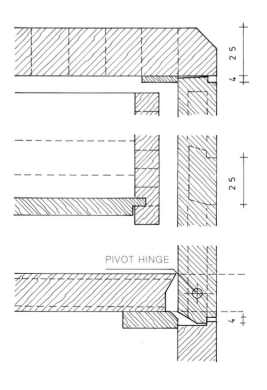

2 5

4

2 5

PIVOT HINGE

4

veet chestnut desk.
e double-sided
oinet, which is con-
cted to both work
oles, turns and can
 adjusted to either
rk position.

The cutouts on the boards of the door fronts are staggered to create a checkerboard design. The boards are held in alignment with concealed splines; dowels ensure uniform spacing of the boards.

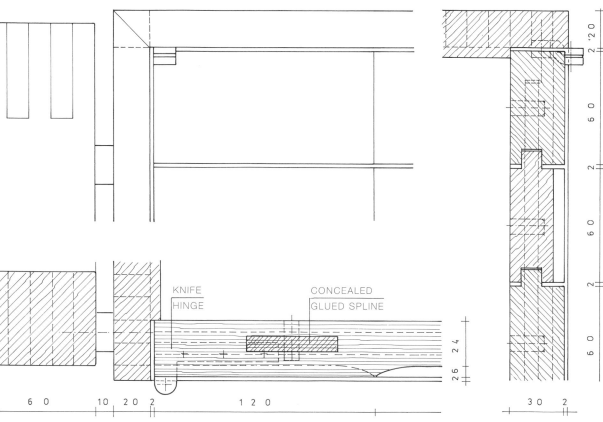

KNIFE
HINGE

CONCEALED
GLUED SPLINE

2 4

2 6

6 0   10 20 2   1 2 0

2 '2 0

6 0

2

6 0

2

6 0

3 0 2

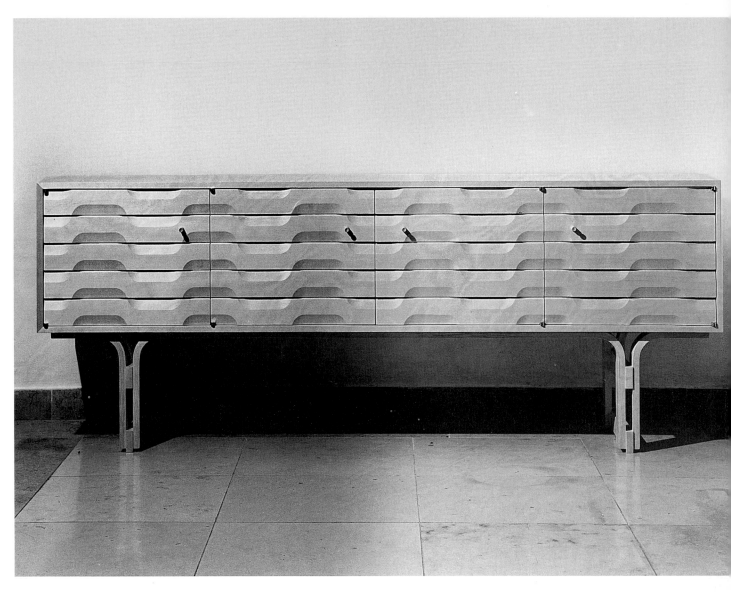

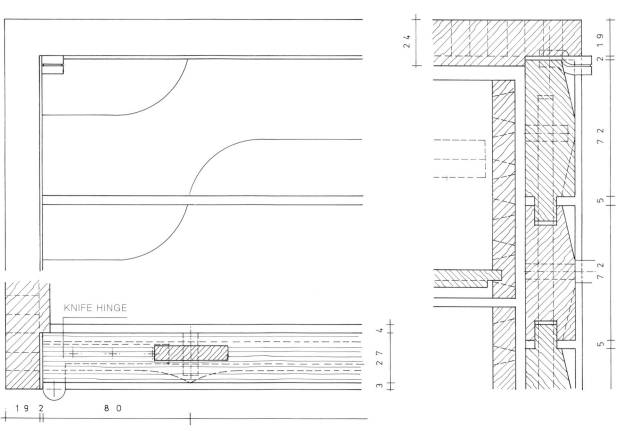

KNIFE HINGE

The wave effect on
the door faces was
created with a router.
The light spruce
used for the piece
accentuates the
beautiful light-and-
shade effect.

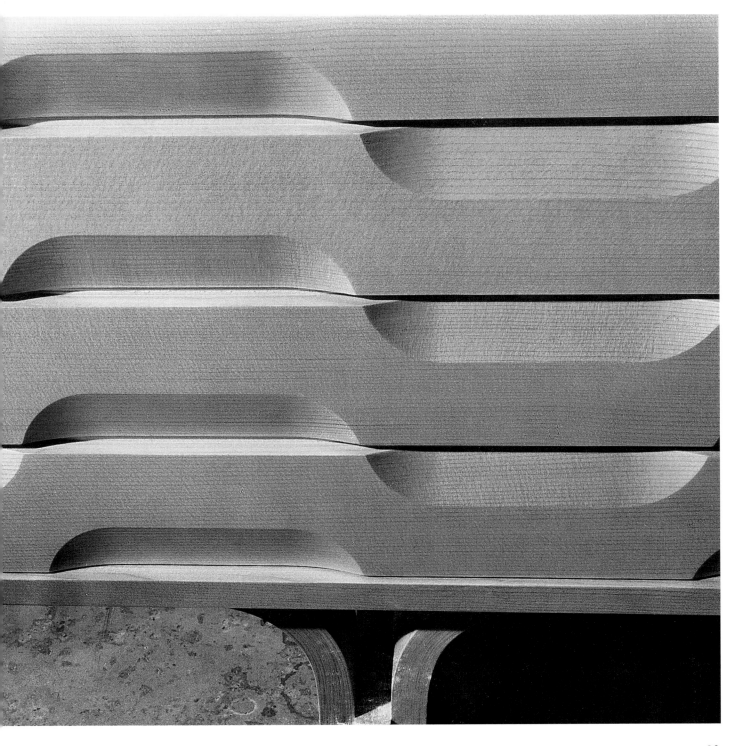

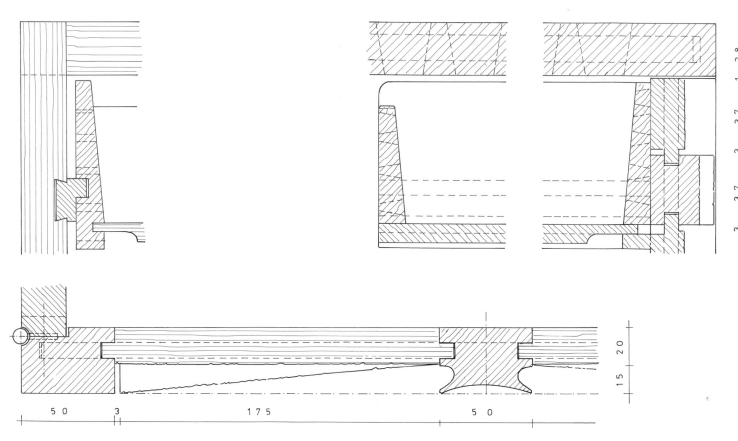

is highly individual
or design was
chieved by using
bered boards split
ong the grain and
ndblasted. Oak is
rticularly well suited
this purpose.

The narrow, tapered
boards of the door
fronts are angled
to create a distinct
impression of depth.
Battens fastened with
dowels on the inside
face reveal how the
doors of this oak
china cabinet were
constructed.

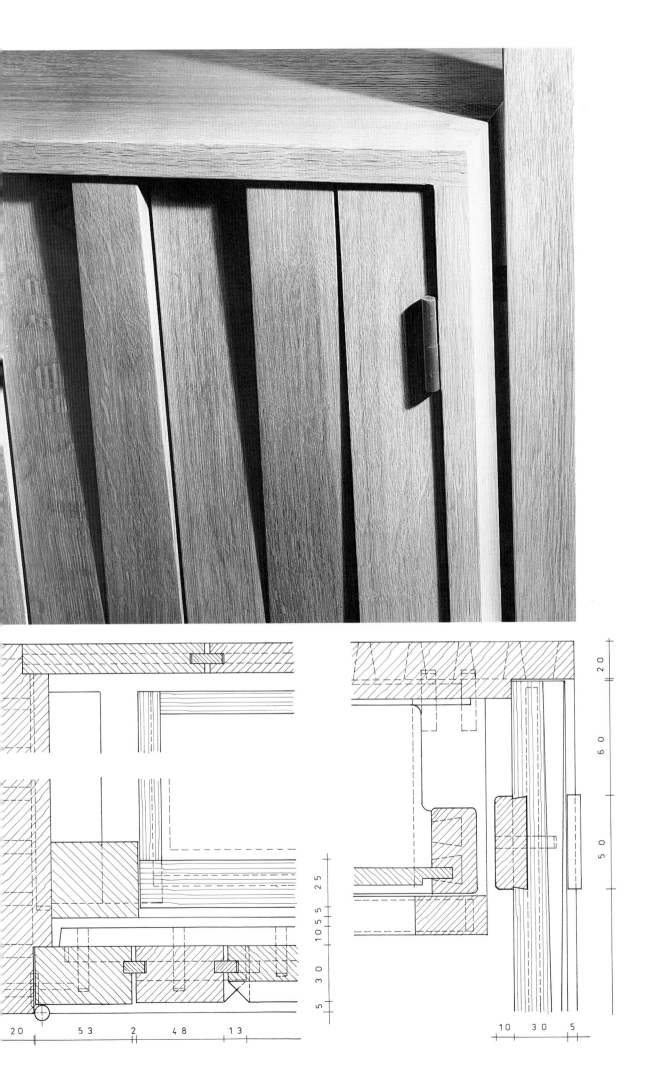

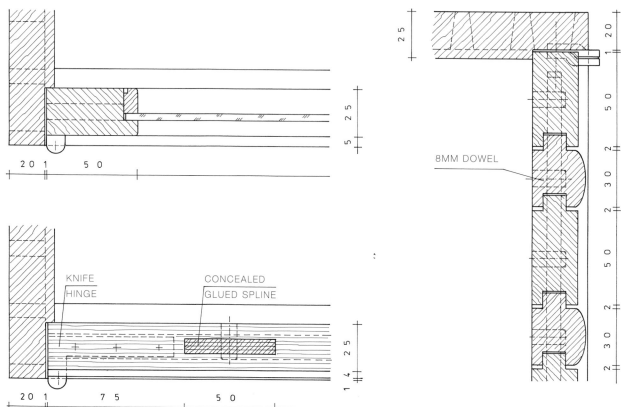

KNIFE HINGE

CONCEALED GLUED SPLINE

8MM DOWEL

e boards of the
oors are held togeth-
 with concealed
lines. Wooden
ndles are built into
e door fronts. Yellow
e (heartwood and
pwood) was used
 this piece.

The cross rails determine the design of the door fronts and provide a surface for mounting the wooden door handles. This cabinet for musical instruments is made of fumed oak.

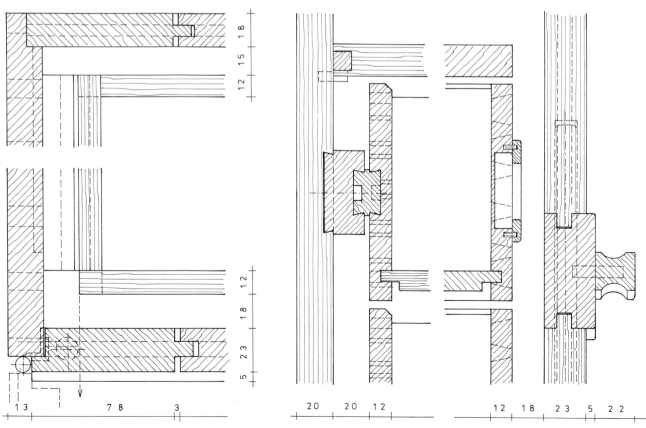

The wooden door handles on this pine cabinet appear to grow from boards in the door fronts. The cabinets are connected to each other and to the supporting framework with dovetail battens.

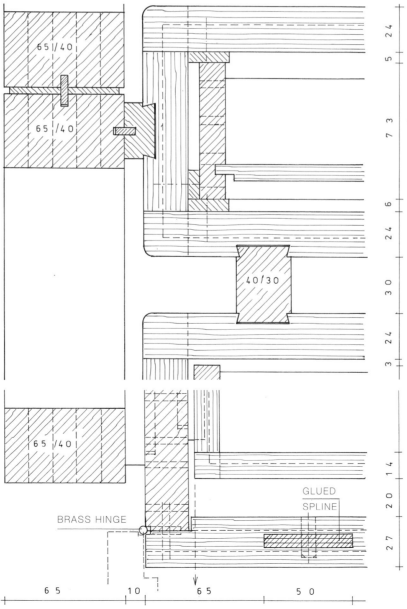

65 /40

65 /40

65 /40

40/30

GLUED
SPLINE

BRASS HINGE

5 24

7 3

24 6

30

3 24

14

20

27

6 5   1 0   6 5   5 0

This ash desk with two side cabinets on wheels illustrates pur board construction. The pedestal feet and inserted splines ensure the stability of the work table. Stiles are used in the construction of the door fronts.

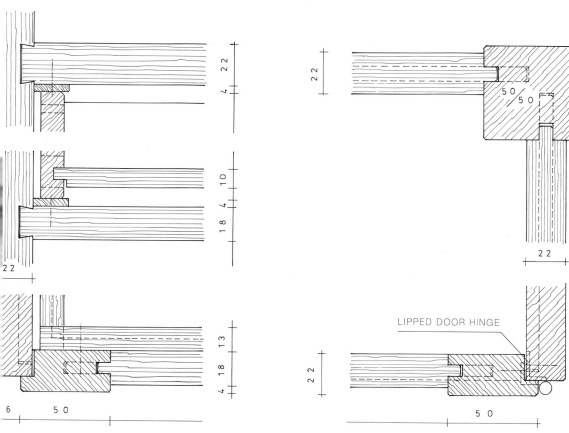

LIPPED DOOR HINGE

41

This oak wardrobe, custom built for a children's room, illustrates profiled board construction. The top and bottom rails extend to form wooden door hinges. The wooden lock mechanism adds to the charm of the piece.

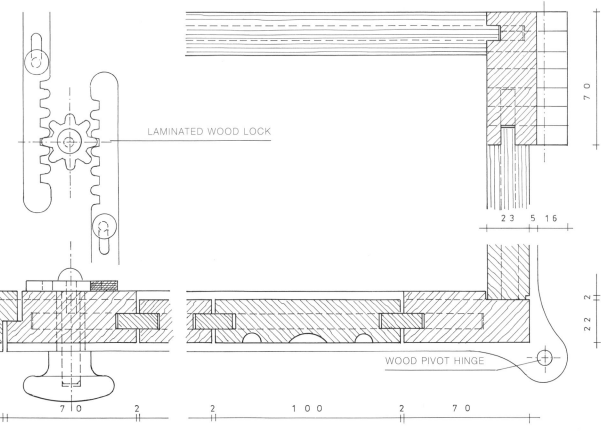

LAMINATED WOOD LOCK

WOOD PIVOT HINGE

70

23 5 16

22 2

70 2

2 100 2 70

43

This china cabinet in pear is an interesting example of board construction. The rails that provide the stability for the doors extend to form wooden hinges. Careful selection of the wood is critical for the functioning of this type of construction.

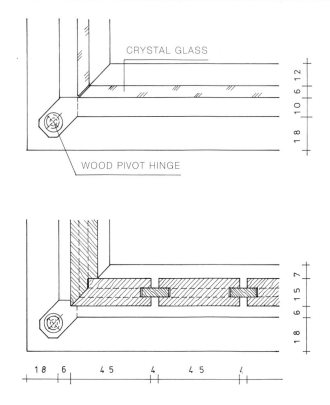

CRYSTAL GLASS

WOOD PIVOT HINGE

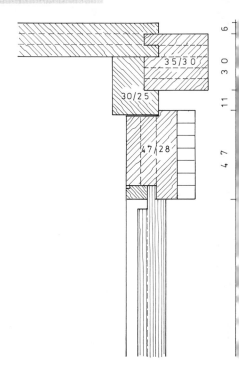

modest liquor
binet in pine. The
usual inclusion of
ergrown pine knots
the panels gives
amusing look to
piece.

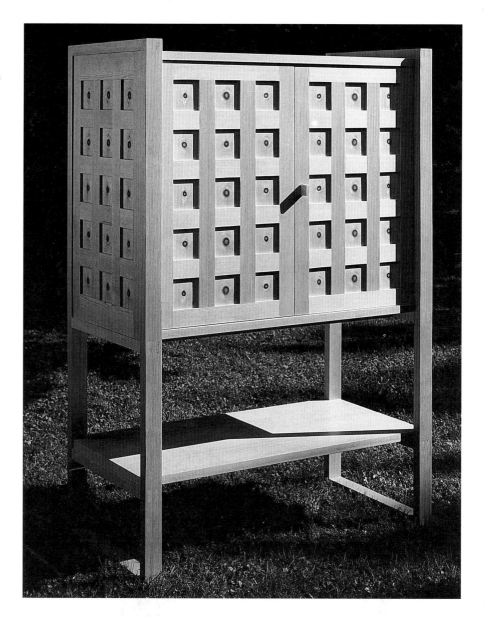

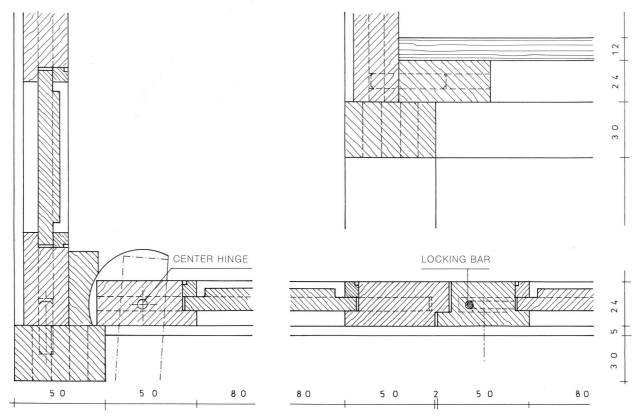

CENTER HINGE

LOCKING BAR

50   50   80

80   50   2   50   80

12

24

30

24

5

30

The door and side
panels of this Douglas
fir document cabinet
are divided up into
narrow friezes,
running diagonally in
part. Fine-grained
wood must be used
to achieve such
an effect.

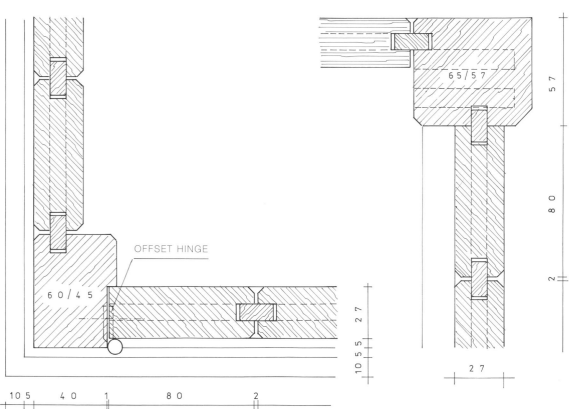

OFFSET HINGE

60 / 45

10 5 5 2 7

10 5   40   1   80   2

65 / 57

5 7

8 0

2

2 7

A modest living-room cabinet of choice beechwood. Two traditional construction features (drawers on full-extension slides and the inclusion of a writing drawer) are incorporated into a modern design.

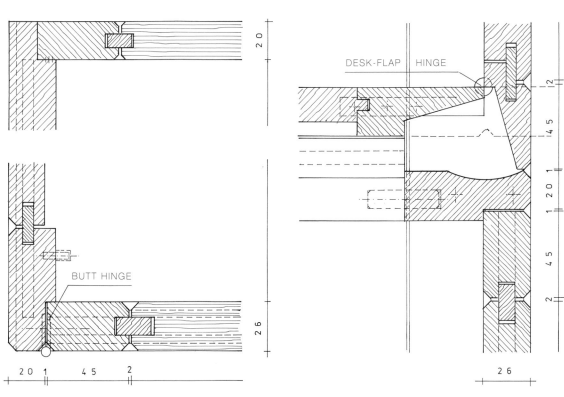

DESK-FLAP HINGE

BUTT HINGE

The drawer slides and wooden bar-lock mechanism are note-worthy features of this glass cabinet in oak.

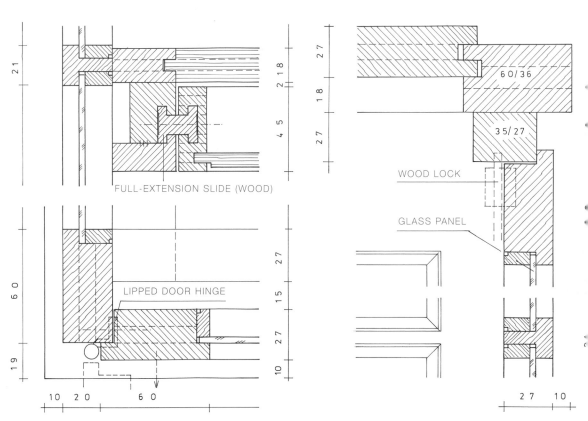

FULL-EXTENSION SLIDE (WOOD)

LIPPED DOOR HINGE

WOOD LOCK

GLASS PANEL

60/36

35/27

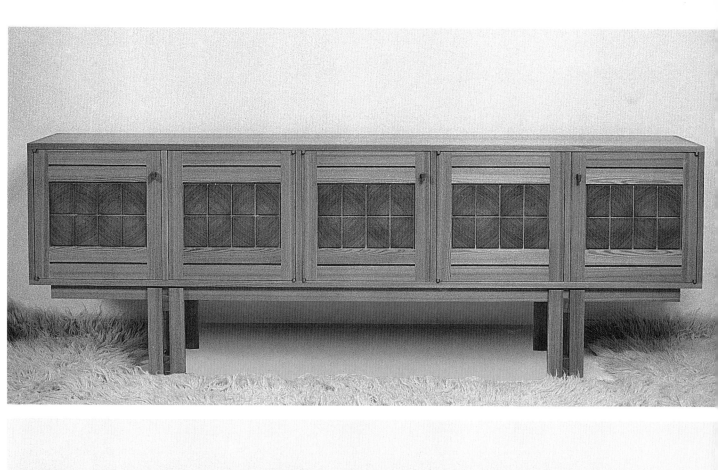

End-grain designs require particularly careful drying of the wood used. In the case of the Larch dresser shown here, choice of wood and careful woodworking are also very important.

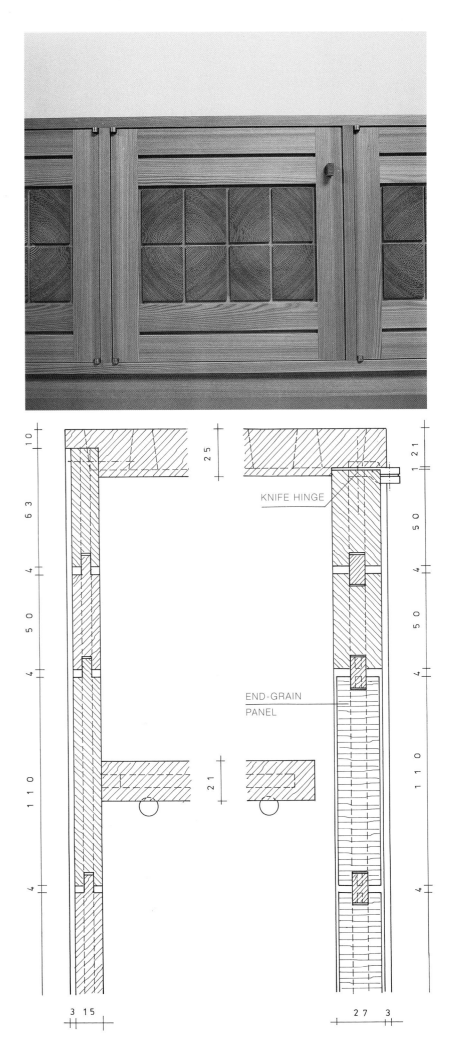

10

2 5

6 3

KNIFE HINGE

4

5 0

5 0

5 0

4

4

END-GRAIN
PANEL

1 10

2 1

1 10

4

4

3 1 5

2 7   3

The corners of this
glass cabinet are
beveled. Fine-grained
spruce was chosen
for the frames, and
beautifully figured
spruce for the panels.

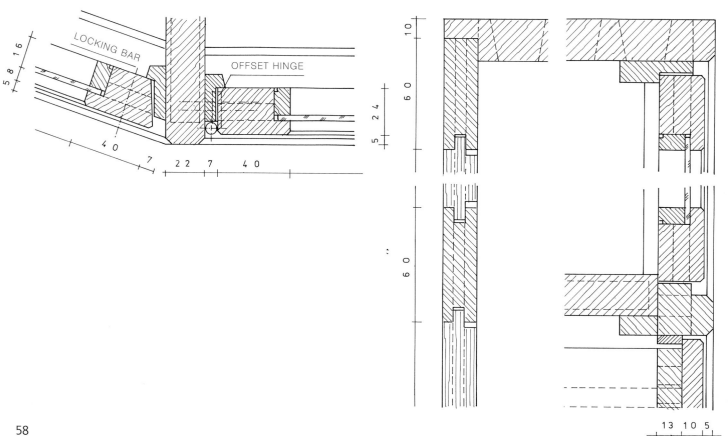

LOCKING BAR

OFFSET HINGE

DRAWER

This larch sideboard shows how effective the combination of fine-grained wood and beautifully figured wood can be. The door handles are also a noteworthy feature of the piece.

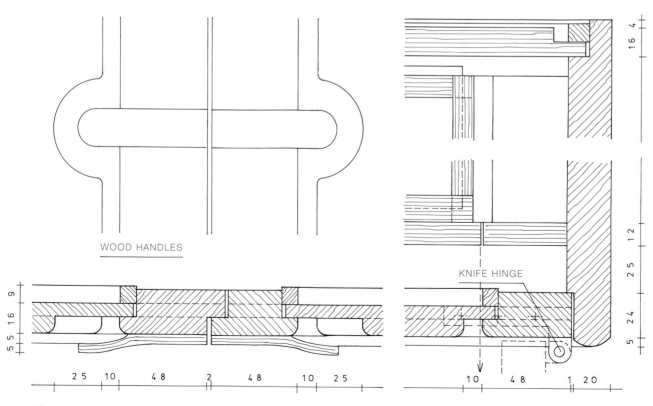

WOOD HANDLES

KNIFE HINGE

The panels of this ash china cabinet are divided up geometrically. An additional design feature is the hollowing out of the small square corner panels.

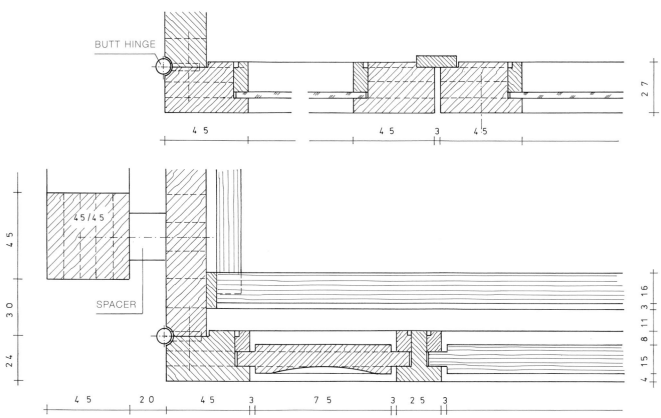

BUTT HINGE

2 7

4 5

4 5 3 4 5

4 5

45/45

3 0

SPACER

2 4

3 16

8 11

4 15 8

4 5 2 0 4 5 3 7 5 3 2 5 3

Novel corner joints
and the partitioning
of the side panels
define the look of this
gun cabinet in ash.

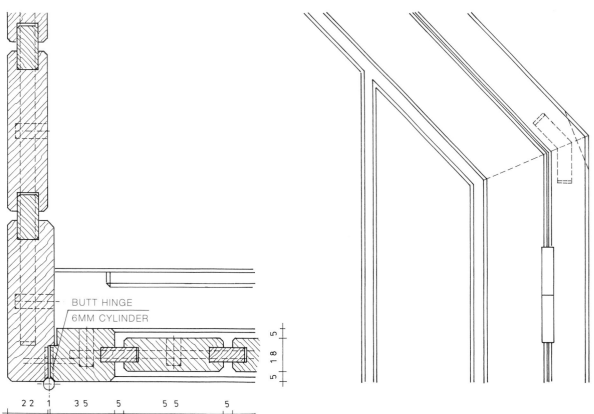

BUTT HINGE
6MM CYLINDER

5 18 5

2 2   1   3 5   5   5 5   5

This plain larch
dining-room cabinet
is noteworthy for
the partitioning of the
panels and the choice
of wood.

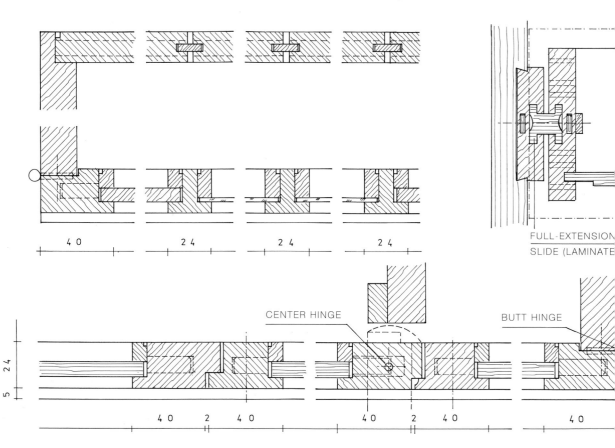

FULL-EXTENSION
SLIDE (LAMINATE)

CENTER HINGE

BUTT HINGE

40   2   40   40   2   40   40

The sides of this two-part china cabinet in spruce are finger-jointed. Full-extension slides are used for the drawers to compensate for the shallow cabinet depth.

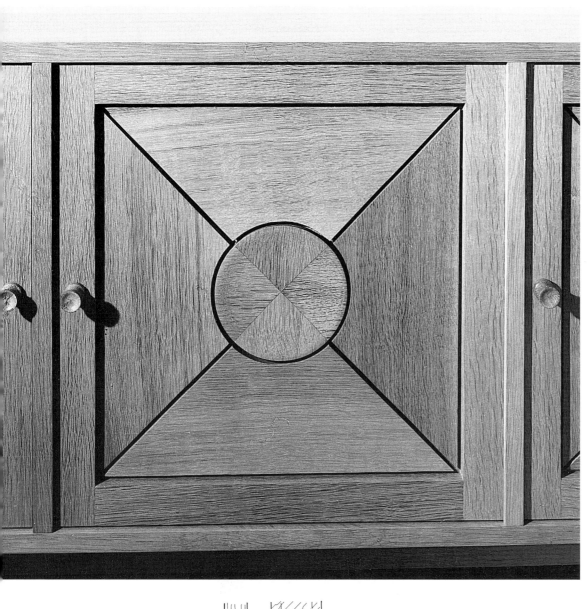

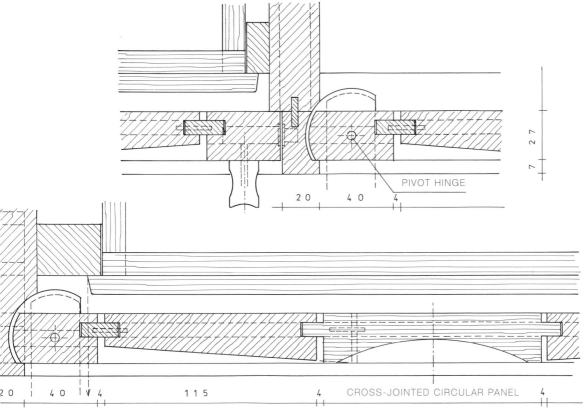

PIVOT HINGE

20   40   4

20   40   4   115   4   CROSS-JOINTED CIRCULAR PANEL   4

7 27

The carcase of this
finger-jointed cabinet
for china and glasses
is Douglas fir; drawers
and drawer slides are
pearwood.

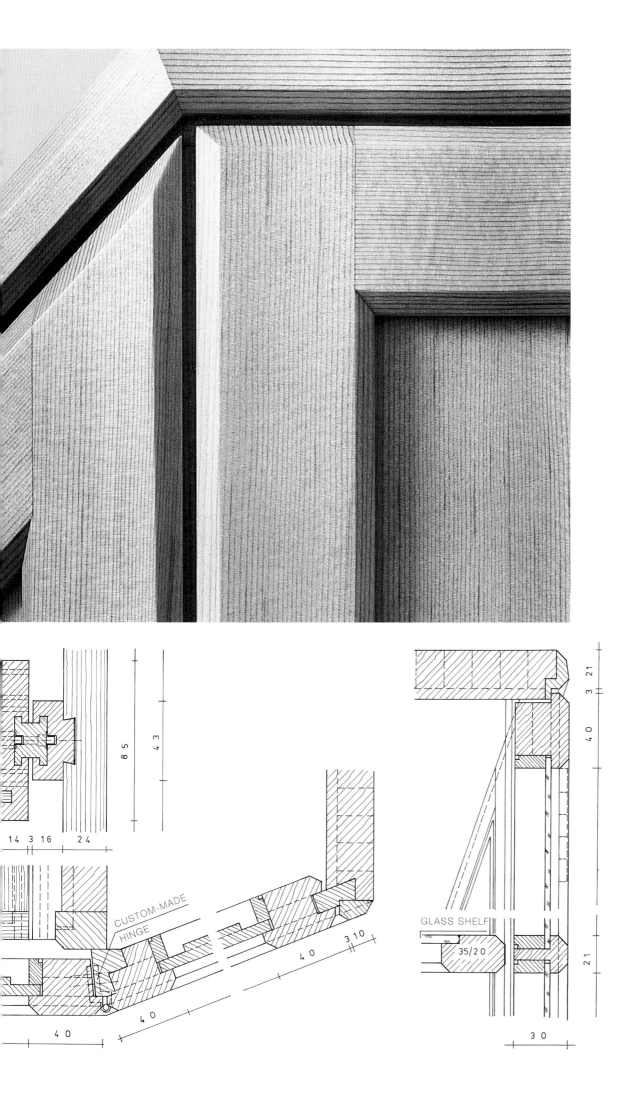

CUSTOM-MADE
HINGE

GLASS SHELF
35/20

When open, the writing leaf of this cherry secretary rests on pegs that protrude from the side cabinets. This means that there's no need for a stay for the drop leaf.

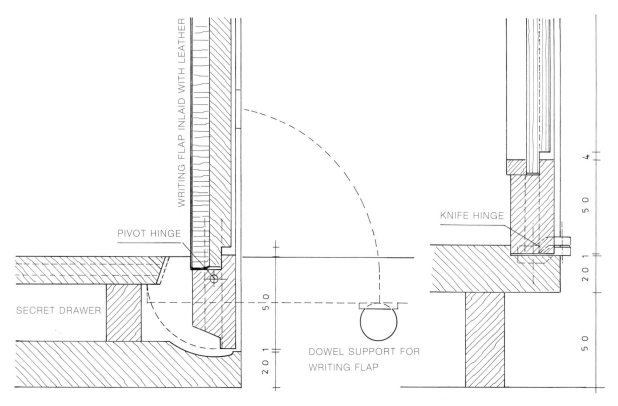

WRITING FLAP INLAID WITH LEATHER

PIVOT HINGE

SECRET DRAWER

KNIFE HINGE

DOWEL SUPPORT FOR WRITING FLAP

2 0 1

5 0

2 0 1

4

5 0

2 0 1

5 0

Fine-grained Douglas fir was used for this glass cabinet. The brass hinges are set in mitered joints and the locking mechanism is of wood. The cornice calls to mind the rustic tradition of furniture making.

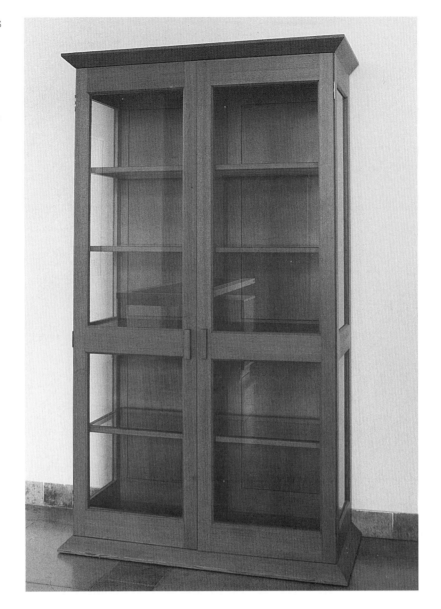

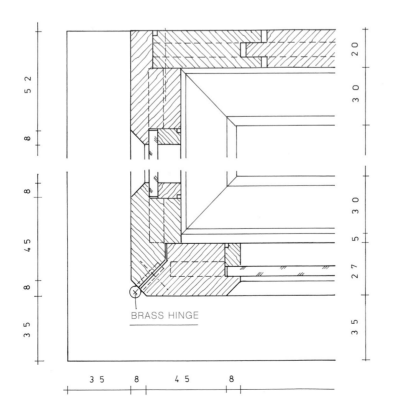

BRASS HINGE

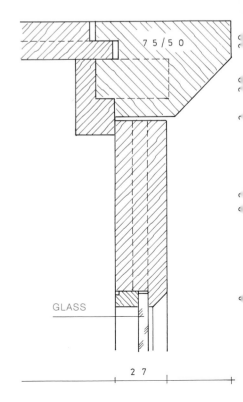

75/50

GLASS

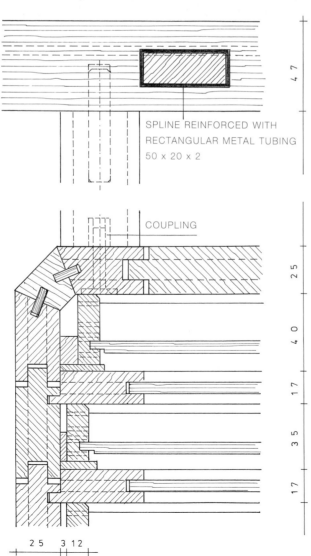

SPLINE REINFORCED WITH
RECTANGULAR METAL TUBING
50 x 20 x 2

4 7

COUPLING

2 5

4 0

1 7

3 5

1 7

2 5   3 1 2

The splines inserted
into the table surface
of this ash desk are
reinforced with rect-
angular metal tubes.
The drawer unit slides
out to provide addi-
tional work space.

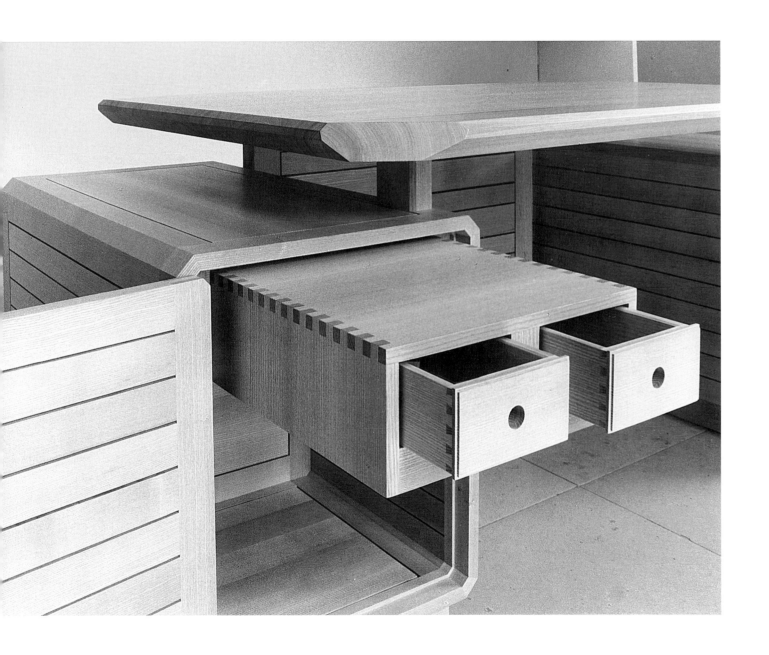

The meandering
pattern on the door
panels of this docu-
ment cabinet is
continued on the
sides. Only fine-
grained wood (in this
case, spruce) can
produce this beautiful
effect; figured wood
would be unsuitable.

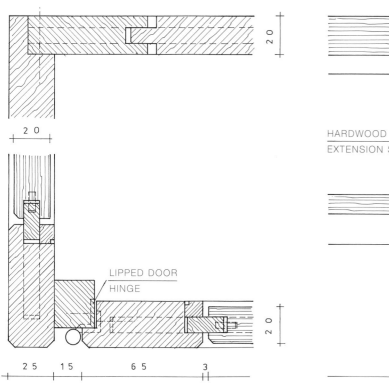

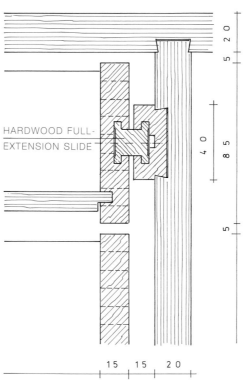

LIPPED DOOR
HINGE

HARDWOOD FULL-
EXTENSION SLIDE

The use of knife hinges provides an interesting construction detail and is consistent with the design of the entire piece. Keyholes are built into the wooden door knobs. Plain pearwood was used for the cabinet.

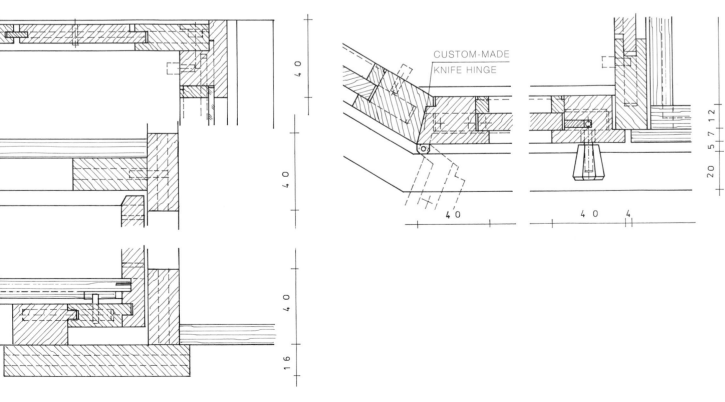

CUSTOM-MADE
KNIFE HINGE

The dovetailed corner joints of this glass china cabinet are a particularly interesting feature. The side door has a concealed lock. Choice spruce was selected for this fine, spare piece.

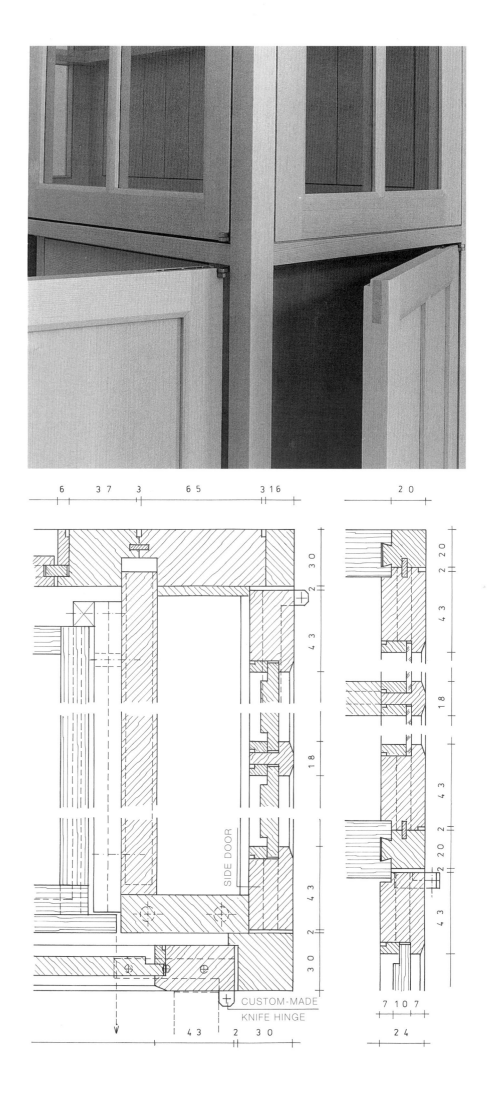

SIDE DOOR

CUSTOM-MADE
KNIFE HINGE

The panel design of the door fronts is repeated on the side of this ash sideboard

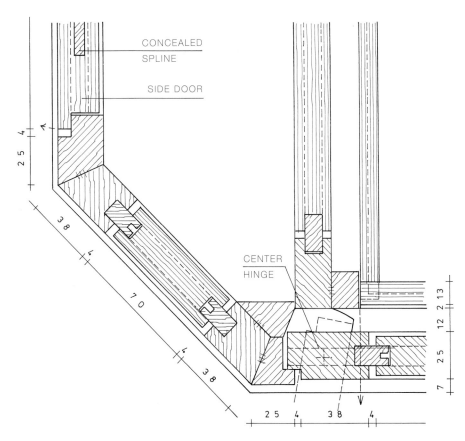

CONCEALED SPLINE

SIDE DOOR

CENTER HINGE

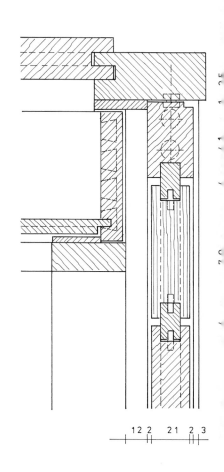

This glass cabinet is
built in such a way
that the bevels open
as part of the doors,
which makes the
inside of the cabinet
more accessible.

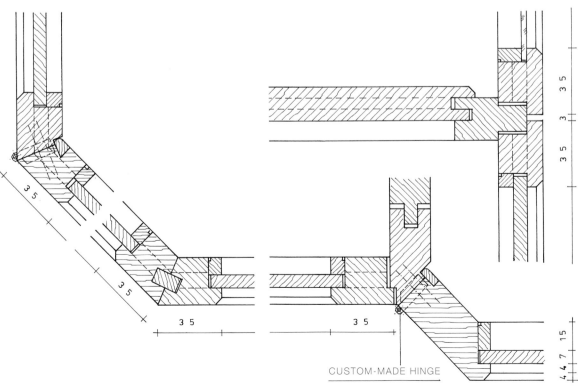

CUSTOM-MADE HINGE

The same panel
design is used on the
cabinet fronts and
case sides of this elm
desk. The use of solid
wood makes it pos-
sible to rout out the
recessed handles.

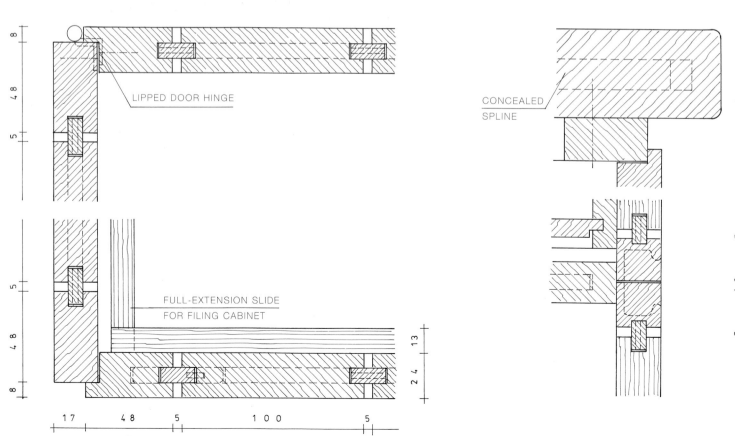

LIPPED DOOR HINGE

CONCEALED
SPLINE

FULL-EXTENSION SLIDE
FOR FILING CABINET

8

48

5

5

48

8

17   48   5   100   5

13

24

5

7

5

48

5

The milled slats of the door panels create a charming play of light in a pale wood such as the ash used here.

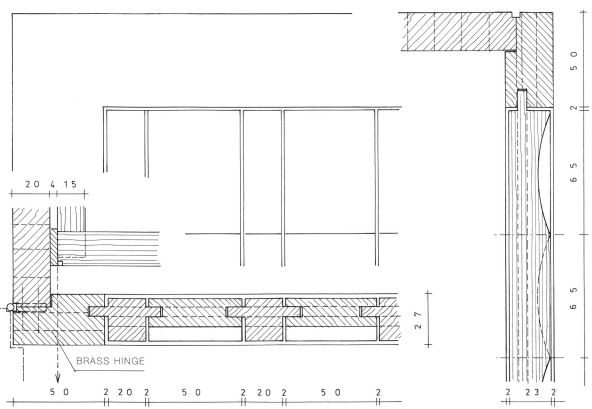

BRASS HINGE

The door-panel design is repeated behind the glass on the back panel of the cabinet. Elm was used for the case.

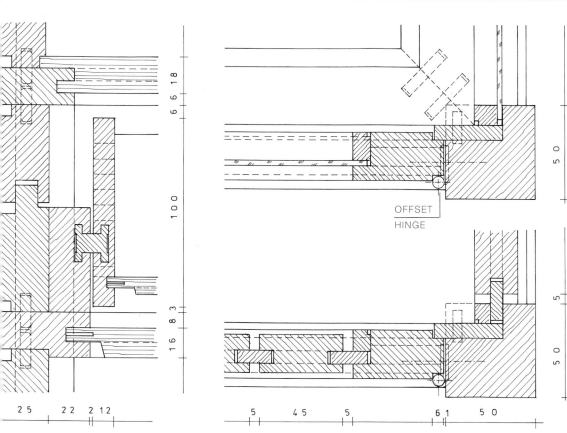

OFFSET
HINGE

The quilted effect on the door fronts of the china cabinet was achieved by milling the panels. A subtle fine-grained wood such as Douglas fir necessary to produce this effect.

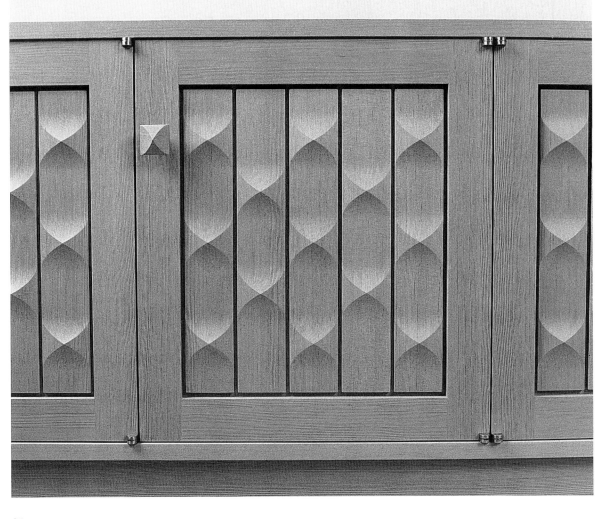

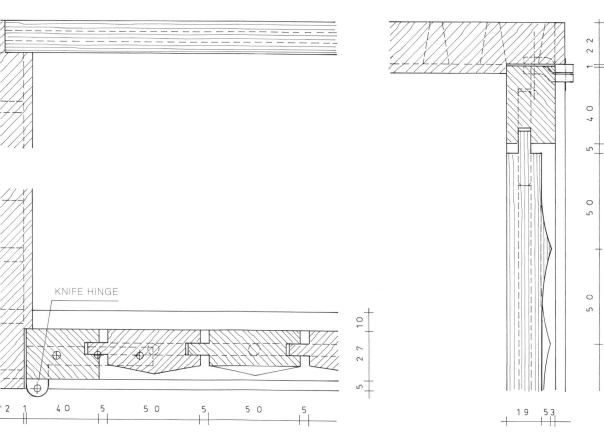

KNIFE HINGE

10
27
5

2 1   40   5   50   5   50   5

1 22
40
5
50
50

19 53

This glass display case features built-in lighting. Because this piece is designed as a freestanding unit, the corners are beveled. The bevels open as part of the doors.

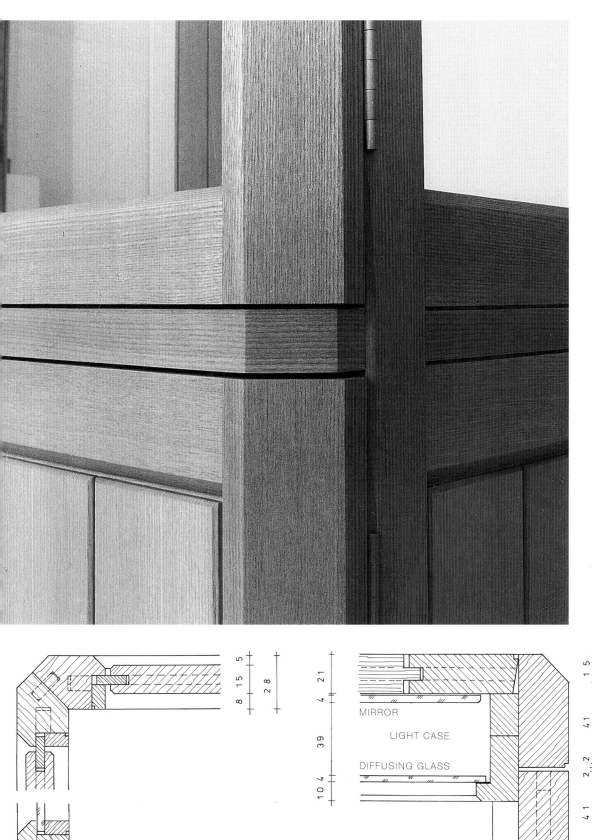

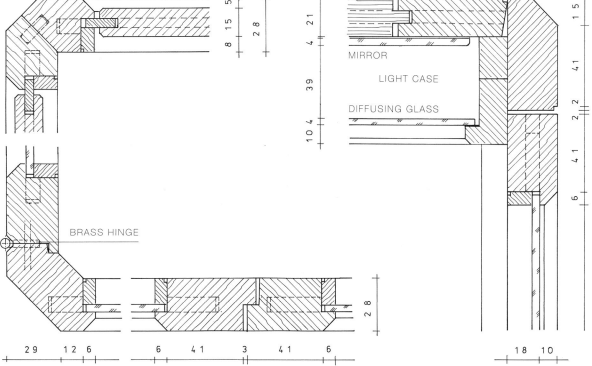

MIRROR

LIGHT CASE

DIFFUSING GLASS

BRASS HINGE

The contrast between the wide, beautifully figured panels and the narrow, chip-carved panels gives this elm photo cabinet its distinctive look.

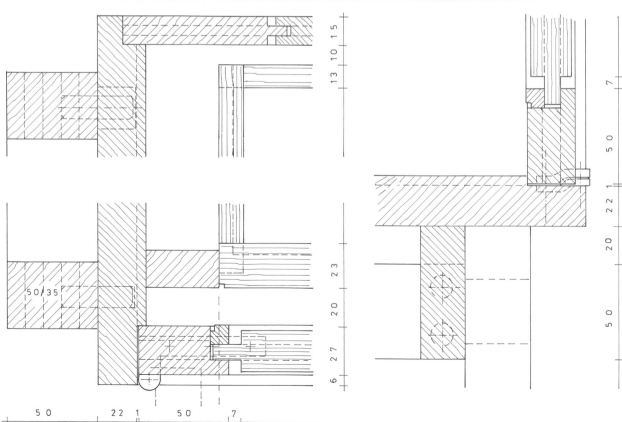

The full-extension slides of the cutlery drawers add to the utility of this ash china cabinet. The piece succeeds because of the harmony of its proportions.

Beautifully figured
cherry boards were
the starting point for
the design of this
china cabinet.

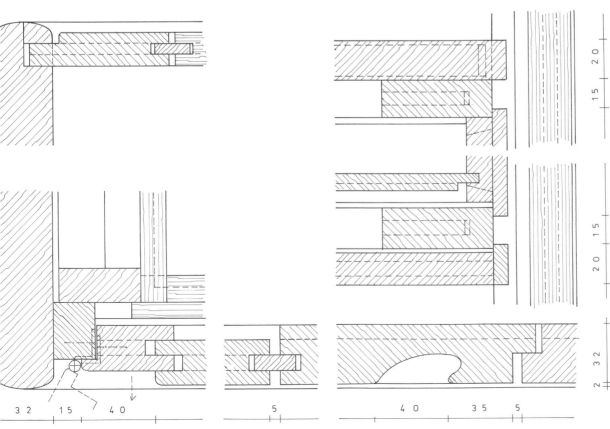

The individual cabinets, which are joined with mortise and tenon, rest on a supporting framework. The piece combines spruce, natural leather and glass.

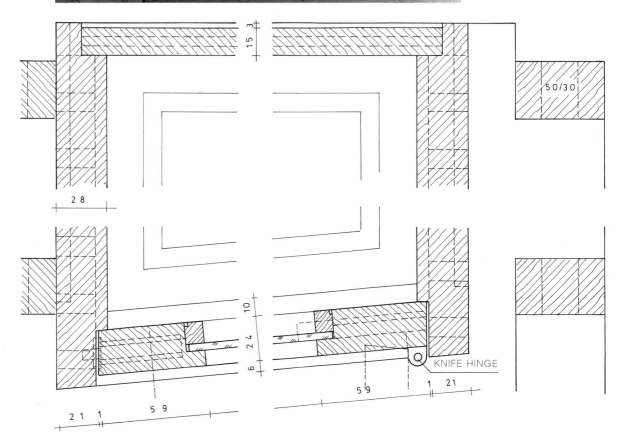

KNIFE HINGE

This plain, rustic
cabinet is made from
spruce and elm.
The beautiful veining
of the door panels
is accentuated by
the modesty of
the construction.

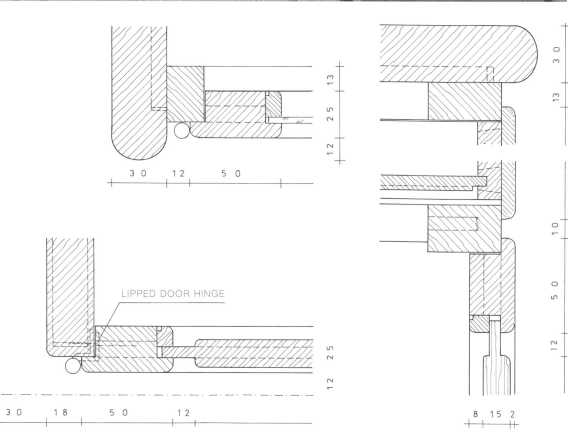

LIPPED DOOR HINGE

115

The individual cabinets are connected with dovetail battens to form a sideboard. The panels consist of tongue-and-grooved boards of differing widths.

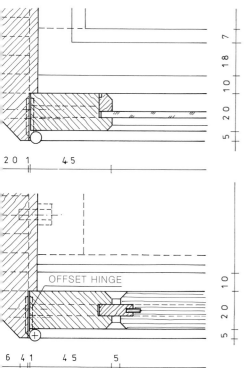

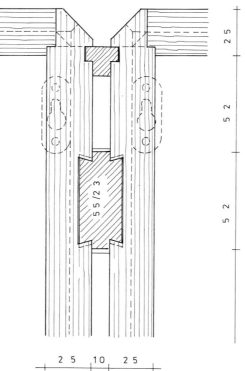

OFFSET HINGE

This document cabinet shows clearly how a lively light-and-shade effect can be created by dividing door fronts into small, flattened panels. The effect is enhanced by the shallower depth of the upper cabinet. A light wood like pine adds to the charm of the piece.

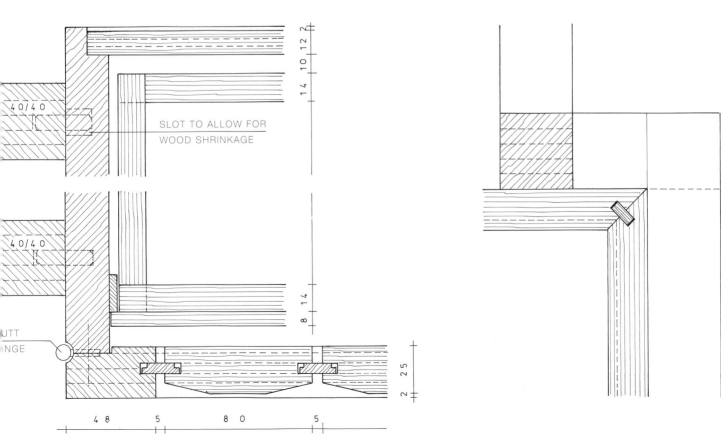

SLOT TO ALLOW FOR
WOOD SHRINKAGE

40/40

40/40

UTT
NGE

48   5   8 0   5

14 10 12 2

8 14

2 2 5

119

End-grain designs
require particular
care, as in the case
of this spruce cabinet.
Perfect results
depend on the selec-
tion and drying of the
wood, the preparation
of the panels and the
surface finish.

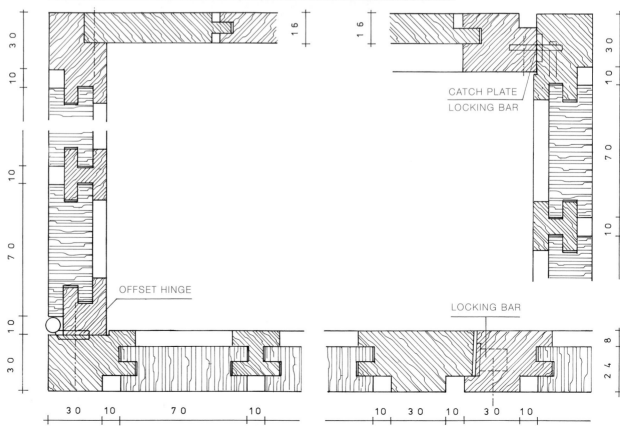

CATCH PLATE
LOCKING BAR

OFFSET HINGE

LOCKING BAR

Post Construction

We more commonly associate the use of posts with the construction of tables and chairs, but they can also be used effectively in cabinetmaking.

Elongated posts or frames support the carca and ensure stability. The posts can be built i the design of a cabinet in a variety of ways.

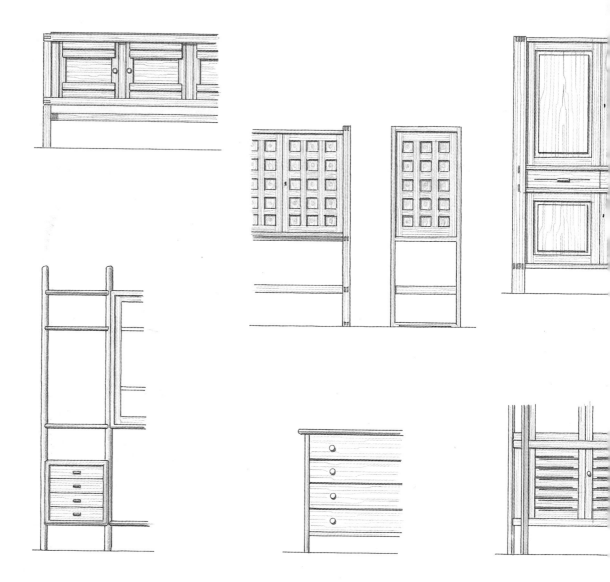

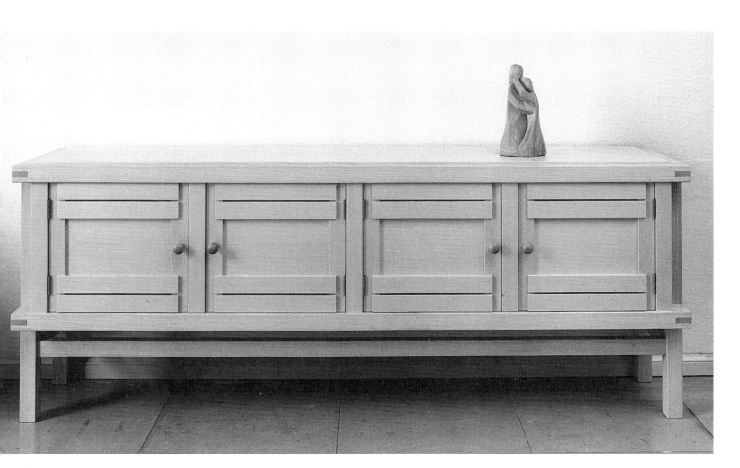

...ariation on post
...nstruction. Fine-
...ined spruce is an
...ropriate choice for
...h a design.

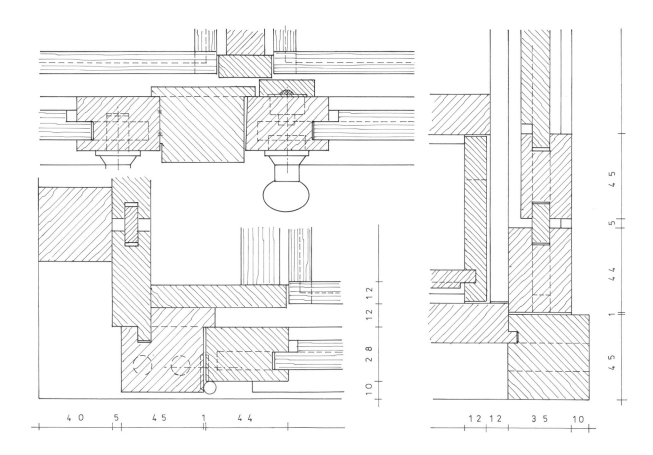

An unusual effect of depth is achieved by using a highly individual panel design. The effect can best be obtained by using light-colored, fine-grained spruce.

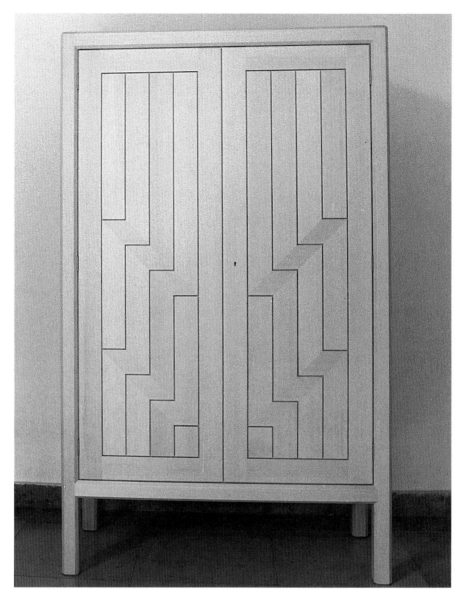

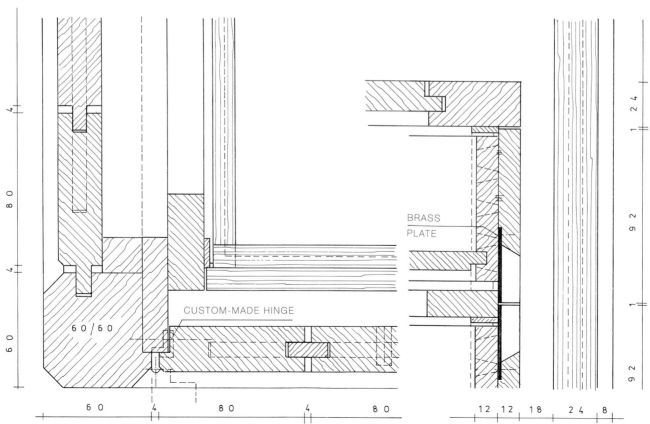

BRASS PLATE

CUSTOM-MADE HINGE

60/60

60   4   80   4   80   12 12   18   24   8

4

80

4

60

1 2 4

9 2

1

9 2

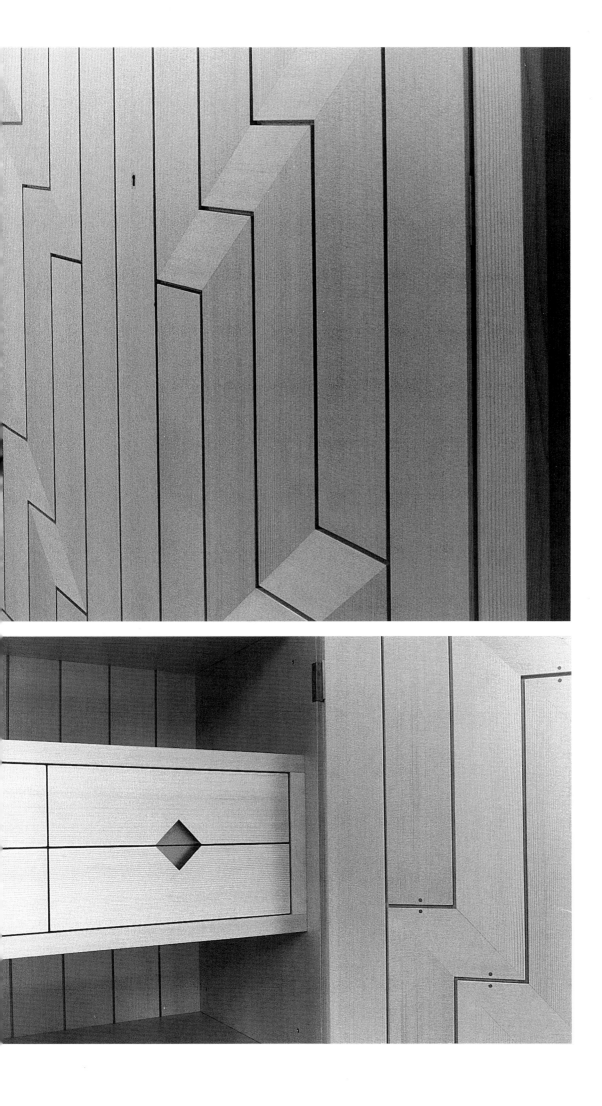

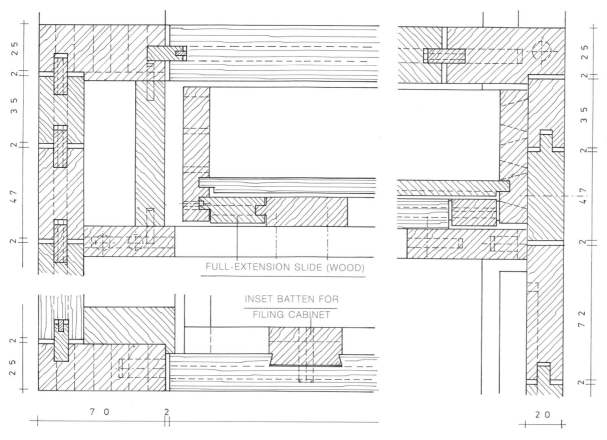

Beech desk. The
through-tenoned
posts (together with
the board panels)
produce the intended
Spartan effect of a
commercial piece of
furniture.

FULL-EXTENSION SLIDE (WOOD)

INSET BATTEN FOR
FILING CABINET

Linen closet in post-construction style. The use of custom-made hinges makes it easy to take the doors off the cabinet.

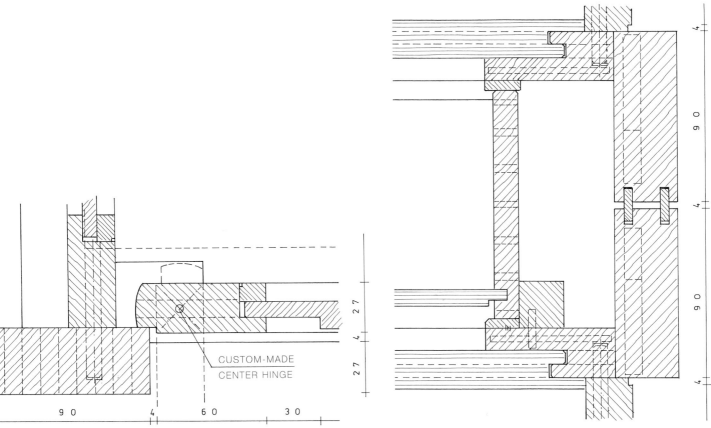

CUSTOM-MADE
CENTER HINGE

9 0   4   6 0   3 0

2 7

4

2 7

4

9 0

4

9 0

4

This commode and wall-hung cabinet feature classic post construction with drawers on full-extension slides. Both pieces are in pearwood.

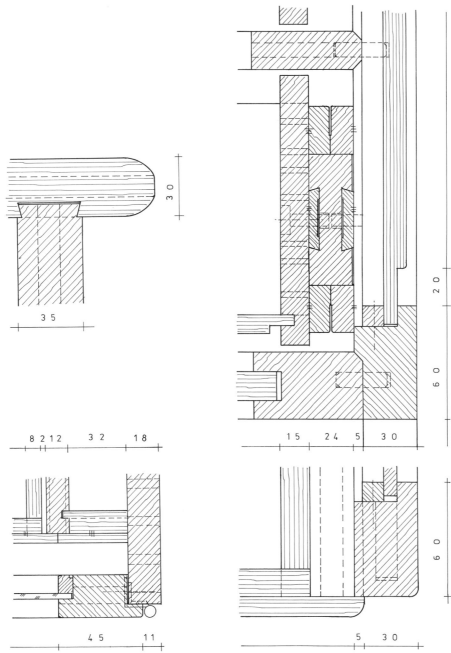

This spruce glass cabinet can be opened from the sides as well as from the front. An interesting wooden locking mechanism complements the piece.

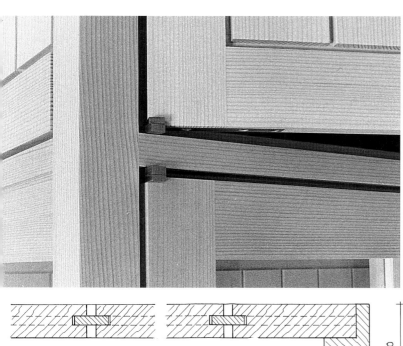

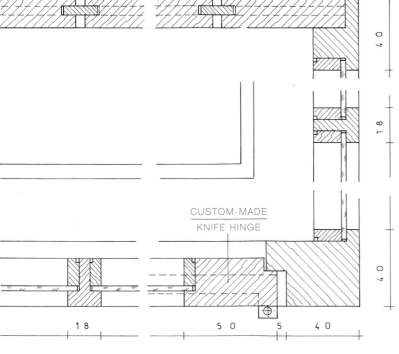

CUSTOM-MADE
KNIFE HINGE

4 0

1 8

4 0

18   5 0   5   4 0

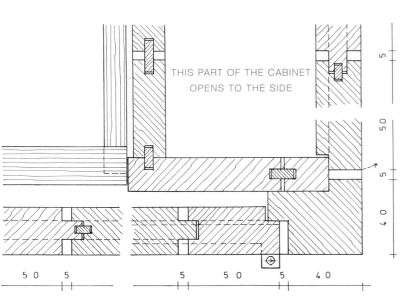

THIS PART OF THE CABINET
OPENS TO THE SIDE

5

5 0

5

4 0

5 0   5   5   5 0   5   4 0

The exposed joints
are a noteworthy
feature of the con-
struction of this gun
cabinet. The small,
hollowed panels
provide a contrast to
the joints.

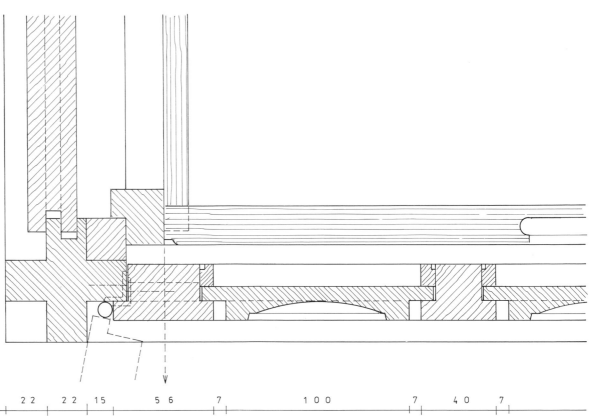

22   22   15   5 6   7   1 0 0   7   4 0   7

134

Oak china cabinet
with beveled corners.
The boards of the
door panels are alter-
nately rabbeted on
facing edges. The oak
is lightly fumed.

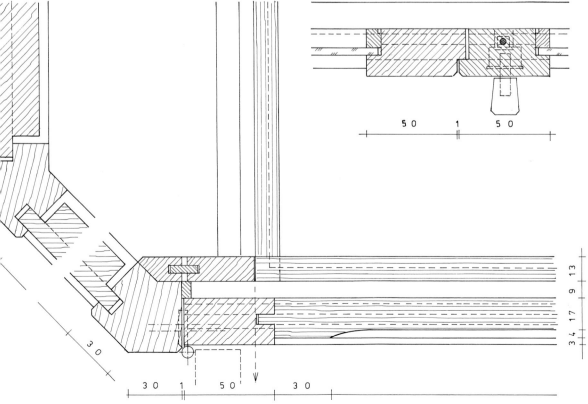

137

The paneled posts provide the necessary stability for this cherry writing desk. The careful choice of wood produces a beautiful effect. The writing leaf is inlaid with leather.

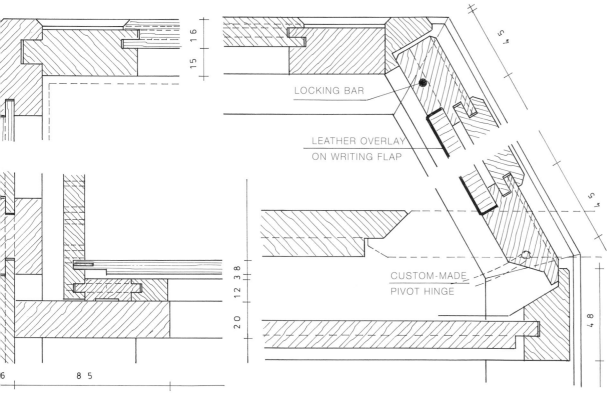

LOCKING BAR

LEATHER OVERLAY
ON WRITING FLAP

CUSTOM-MADE
PIVOT HINGE

A charming piece,
combining post con-
struction and "build-
ing-block" design.
Removable wood
screws allow adjust-
ment of this ash
bookcase to suit
different functions.

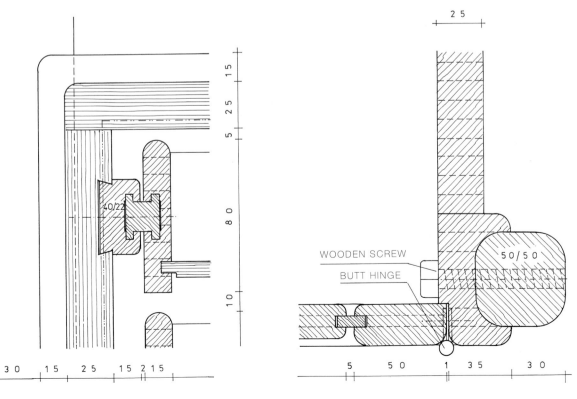

WOODEN SCREW

BUTT HINGE

50 / 50

40/2?

25

15 25 5 80 10

30 15 25 15 2 15

5 50 1 35 30

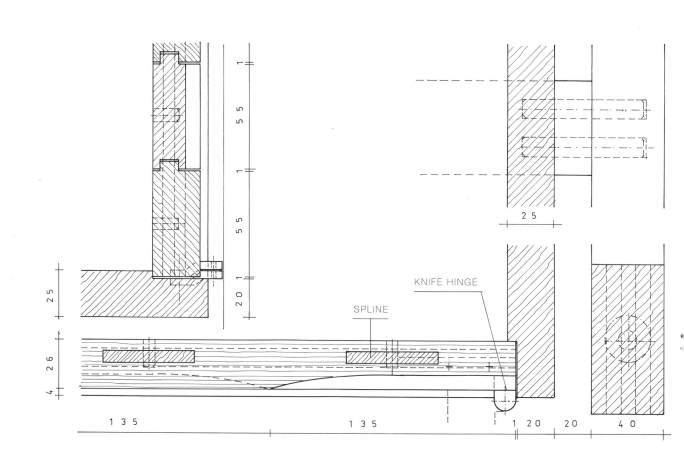

KNIFE HINGE

SPLINE

sk in light-colored
n with leather
ting surface. The
ards of the cabinet
es are alternately
ted, which makes
ossible to build the
oden handles into
boards.

The pieces shown in this book were made by:

Photographs:

Bauer, Roland, 7176 Braunsbach
BM-Redaktion, 7022 Leinfelden-Echterdingen
Karg, Franz, 8100 Garmisch-Partenkirchen
Kölbl, Franz, 8100 Garmisch-Partenkirchen